A Shortcut to Success

*3 Ancient Secrets
to
Getting Ahead
and
Creating an Amazing Life*

Bob Huttinga, PA-C

Acknowledgments

With the influence of the following people and many others, I have been able to create the amazing life that I currently experience. These are men and women who helped form my thinking and helped me awaken to my own creative abilities.

My wife and business partner, Barbara Kaye Huttinga
My parents, Alko and Alice Huttinga

Mentors: Drs. Bruce Bennett, Richard Yerian, John London,
Mentors: Drs. Caesar Bonet, Robert Painter, and Grant Born
Mentor Arnold Blanksma
Mentor Louis Barbone

Author Jose Silva
Author Napoleon Hill
Author Richard Bach
Author Wayne Dyer
Author Kevin Trudeau
Author Louise Hay
Author Neville Goddard
Author David Gicandi
Author Hamid Bey
Author Lee Carroll

Dedication

I dedicate this book to the seekers, producers, and workers who are actively creating their lives. This book is also dedicated to the followers and drifters who will one day awaken and become responsible for creating their own lives.

Author's Note

This book is short and simple. It is not my intention to spend a lot of time trying to convince you that you can change your life by changing your thinking. If you are a seeker, you probably already know that. If you are looking for a method to get ahead faster, here is something that will work consistently.

I have spent 35 years working this method out and have used it successfully for a number of years, so now I can create what I desire in my life. Does this method work 100 percent the first time? No!

I have found that if it does not work immediately there are only two possible reasons. 1. Some memory from the past is holding you back, or 2. You are not thinking correctly about the future. The solutions to this are clearly explained in the book and will be easy for you to understand and implement.

How long does it take to create an amazing life? Actually, it will take a lifetime. Once you learn to use this formula, you will continue to use it to create whatever you desire. Your desires will change as your belief in your ability to create gets greater and greater. The journey of your life will be amazing with one "unbelievable" coincidence after another.

You will soon know how to successfully create whatever you desire to be, to do, and to have.

—Bob Huttinga PA-C

Disclaimer

The pages of this book contain many recommendations. To the best of my knowledge, the things that I have written about are time-tested suggestions that I have compiled in a unique manner. There are many more wonderful tools that I have chosen not to explore in these pages. These are only suggestions. It is up to you to use them to get ahead and create an amazing life. You are responsible. You are the writer, designer, producer, performer, star, and actor in your own life. It is up to you to take these suggestions and use them with common sense. I am your coach. If something I say does not make sense to you, you can disregard it, research it, or discuss it with a professional who is qualified in that area. Only use these suggestions if they resonate with your own thinking. You can create an amazing life. Here are some great tools.

Contents

1

Introduction

Success is the progressive realization of a worthwhile goal. This is the definition given to us by Napoleon Hill. Many of us have success in a part of our lives but not in other parts. Some have great business success but have poor relationships. Others have a great marriage but experience poverty. I know people who have never been on a vacation or seen any of the amazing beauty in our world while others travel and engage with people in other cultures.

What is your life like today?

Are you living a full and happy life?

Is every part of your life working, or are there some parts that could be better?

Do you have fears, anxiety, depression, anger, frustration, resentment, jealousy, disappointment, or other unhealthy emotions?

What would your life be like if every part—relationships, finances, career, health, and recreation—all worked well together, and you were completely happy all the time?

Wow. Think about that for a moment. What would that *look* like; what would that *sound* like; what would that *feel* like?

My name is Bob Huttinga. My wife, Barb, and I operate The Healing Center in Lakeview, Michigan. I have spent my entire adult life searching for answers to a few simple but profound questions: "What is my purpose?" "What am I doing here on this Earth?" I know that I am not alone in this search. Every person who is reading this book is also a searcher, trying to make sense of things. We all want our lives to have some meaning.

I recall asking my parents many questions about the meaning of life. I do not recall hearing any satisfactory answers. Most of the time, their answers were based on our Christian faith. They would say, "God will provide, and you do not have to worry about it." Even as a small child, I could not accept that kind of thought. I wanted to understand.

In my search, I have had several important milestones. Born into a very religious family, I was raised with a strong background in Christianity. My parents provided me with a base of good morals and a work ethic that I appreciate very much. We were never taught about goal-setting. When we wanted something, we were instructed to pray about it and add, "Not my will, but thine be done." Then, we were to wait and watch, hoping or expecting to receive miraculous results.

Actually, this turned me into an opportunist. The prayer really was a form of goal-setting, although I did not realize that at the time. This lack of initial realization is why I will spend some time, later in this book, discussing goal setting and how you can recognize a great opportunity when it knocks.

The next milestone in my life was becoming a physician assistant. From age 12, after having had a minor injury, I wanted to be a doctor. However, the negative programming I received as a child caused me to doubt that I had the necessary financial and intellectual resources to get through medical school. In spite of average grades in college, I was accepted into the Physician Assistant (PA) program at Western Michigan University in Kalamazoo, Michigan. Although I doubted that I could become a doctor, the new profession of PA seemed believable. Due to a great willingness to learn, I graduated with honors from PA school in 1976.

Another big turning point for me was the book *Think and Grow Rich* by Napoleon Hill. Someone gave this book to me when I was 28 years old. It was my first awakening. For the first time in my life, I understood that I did not have to pray and just wait for the opportunity to appear. I learned, instead, that I could pray, and then I could *do something* to make my prayers come true. I could create a life of my own choosing!

The next fork in the road was an introduction to The Silva Method of Mind Development and Stress Control. With this being another first for me, I realized that I could use my mind in a special way to reduce the effects of stress on my body and put my brain into a special state that would promote creativity, healing, and much, much more. It became clear that Jose Silva had created a teachable system for controlling stress and purposefully using the mind to help make life better.

I used this method to normalize high blood pressure and to heal an ulcer, which had developed as the result of a very stressful professional life. Later, I began to practice on other aspects of life. I learned how to find a different job with much better income. I used this method to find a great, reliable used car and to help my children relax while taking tests in school. I was able to achieve many remarkable outcomes that constantly reinforced my new belief that I could use my mind to create a better life, and I experienced a peace of mind that I have never had before.

This Silva Method was so profound and had such an impact on me that I became a Silva Method instructor and taught this method for eight years while working full time as a physician assistant. I used this method to make my life more successful and helped many others do the same. It worked very well for many years, yet I still felt that something was missing. Life was not exactly what I desired because I still did not really understand how creating a life worked. So I continued searching, studying many subjects, reading hundreds of books, listening to many audio programs, and attending lectures on a wide variety of topics.

Another awakening came a few years ago when a friend, Lee Carroll, author of *Indigo Children* and the *Kryon Writings*, provided me with more understanding. He said that people on Earth generally operate in one of three paradigms or according to one of three patterns or models: the Law of Karma, the Law of Grace, and the Law of Co-creation.

The Law of Karma relates to reincarnation, which is the belief of about 70 percent of Earth's population. The concept is that we live many lifetimes. In each lifetime, the events in our lives are determined by happenings from previous lifetimes that we are here to correct during this current lifetime. Events that occur in this lifetime are lessons to be learned, scores to be settled, or debts to be paid. Under the Law of Karma, life is like a rudderless boat with no sail and no engine, just floundering, pushed about by every passing storm and current.

The Law of Grace is the concept best described by the Christian teaching, "Let go and let God." This is a philosophy often promoted by Alcoholics Anonymous and is the belief system with which I was born and raised. The essential thought is: "Give your cares and problems to God then relax and wait for Him to create your life for you." This is like being in a boat with sails and power, but God is at the helm, and you are sitting back, watching life unfold around you and, perhaps, wishing for a better outcome.

The Law of Co-creation applies to how we use the power of God, Spirit, or the Universe to create an outcome that we have in mind. In this model, God is not some great entity outside of ourselves; rather, God is the awareness of being that resides within each of us. When we say the words, "I am," we become aware of our inner awareness of being. This awareness of being is actually the spiritual being that is housed within and around our physical body. Understand that the size of this spiritual being may be very large, perhaps even infinite. It is the vital force that powers up our system. This paradigm is like a boat with sails and an engine with you *and* God at the helm, working together to direct the unfoldment of your life in the way you desire it to be.

We can think of the Law of Co-creation with this metaphor: let's imagine you are hiking in the mountains, and you pick up a rock and take it home. That rock is no longer part of the mountain, yet not one atom of its substance has changed. Changing the rock's location has changed how we view it—as a rock rather than part of a mountain—but the true nature of the rock is still the same. In this paradigm, we are the rock and God is the mountain. We are not the God of *the* universe; we are the god of our own universe.

"When you blame others, you give up your power to change." — Dr. Robert Anthony

---

Many books have been written on the concept of grace, so I will not deal with that here. Karma also is a topic for other venues. My focus is on co-creation and, frankly, that leaves no time for esoteric discussion of either grace or karma because co-creation supersedes both and literally makes them void. The meat of this book will be how to use the power of God and your mind *together* to create an amazing life that will, at times, leave you breathless with wonder at the things that you and God have created.

At The Healing Center, we have a slogan "Put Your Health in Your Own Hands—Healing Body, Mind, and Spirit." As a searcher, I have trained myself in all these areas. With reference to the body, I am trained in traditional medicine as a certified physician assistant (PA-C) with a focus on prescription medications and surgery. In addition to that, I have 20 years of experience in natural medicine, homeopathy, herbs, essential oils, and supplements, and am a certified natural health practitioner (CNHP).

After learning to use the Silva Method, I continued mind/mental training and became a certified hypnotist. I studied Neurolinguistic Programming (NLP) and energy medicine, becoming a level three Reiki master.

For my spiritual training, I have explored the foundations of all major religions with extensive emphasis on the works of Hamid Bey, who was trained in the temples of Egypt. There, he learned the teachings of Christ, which came to Egypt directly from Israel without the contaminating influences of the Greeks and Romans. Bey learned to master his own body. He could put himself into suspended animation and, to prove this ability, was buried alive over 5,000 times, re-emerging from each internment unharmed.

Thanks to these various studies, my focus has been honed to the holistic balance of body, mind, and spirit and learning to use all three in my life and my daily work as a Physician Assistant.

One of my mentors, Dr. Bruce Bennett, said, "Some doctors are healers, and some are technicians. You must learn to be both." I have learned to be both. However, today, for this book, I am a teacher.

In my first book, *Put Your Health in Your Own Hands*, I share the story of a 103-year-old man who came to the Urgent Care where I was working. This man was very healthy. He was on no medications. He had cut his finger working in his workshop and had driven himself to the clinic to get some stitches.

As I repaired the laceration, we talked and I asked him, "What is the secret to your long and healthy life?"

"I stayed away from you dang doctors," was his reply.

We laughed loudly, but there is some truth to this. I did try to explain to him that I was not a doctor but a physician assistant. He did not care as long as I knew how to repair his finger.

Today, I find many people who express the same feeling of dissatisfaction with traditional medicine. This is why I have written these two books: to give you tools to get through your life without being unnecessarily dependent upon others all the time. We often need help and advice, but we must learn to be more independent and responsible for ourselves.

The idea for this book came from another patient who came in for a general physical examination. As I was taking her history, she stated, "I have an amazing, magical life!"

"What does that mean?" I asked.

"Well," she said, "I love my work. I have perfect health. I have many great relationships. I am happy all the time. I feel good all the time. And I have accomplished every goal that I have ever set."

Now, that does sound like an amazing life. It sounds almost too good to be true. And because of past programming from our early family and religious life, most of us will think, "If it sounds too good to be true, it probably is not true." So, people tend to be cautiously optimistic about the idea of co-creating an amazing life.

The great philosopher Socrates once said, "It is the nature of an entity that determines what it can do and what it will do." For example, it is the nature of a wheel to roll easily; however, it is not the nature of a block to roll easily. This concept means that if one human being can do something, any other human being can learn to do it also. It is in our *human* nature to be able to do those things that can help us get ahead quickly and create an amazing life.

If my patient could create an amazing life, anyone and everyone can have an amazing life. If Hamid Bey could control his body, slow down his heart and breathing to be buried alive for many hours, sometimes days, it should be easy for us to learn to be healthy, to lower our blood pressure, control our blood sugars and weight, and heal our ulcers.

The key to all of this is based on how we think. The great Earl Nightingale, co-founder of Nightingale Conant Corporation that produces many motivational tapes and CDs, once said that the greatest secret in the world is, "We become what we think about most of the time."

"The elevator to success is out of order. You'll have to use the stairs...one step at a time." — Joe Girard

---

Several people have told me that there is no shortcut to success. They say that you have to learn from your mistakes and failures until you gain enough wisdom to gradually piece together your dominating thoughts into the things that you desire. This is true; however, is it not also true that if we had learned some secrets earlier in our lives we could have and probably would have gone around some of those obstacles and avoided a lot of pain and loss?

In the next chapter, I will begin the process of teaching you the steps to think correctly so you, too, can create an amazing life easier, sooner, and with joy.

2

My understanding
of how things work

If it is true that we become what we think about most of the time, we must monitor our thoughts. Humans are the only species who can do this. Tielhard DeChardan, in the *Phenomenon of Man,* referred to this as the ability to reflect. All other animals can think; however, we are the only ones who can think about thinking.

Before we go further, it is important to understand that every thought is really two thoughts. Our first thought is whatever we desire, and our second is, too often, our fear that we will not get it. These two thoughts are balanced on the ends of a teeter-totter. Whichever one has the greater mass determines what we experience in our lives.

After reading *Think and Grow Rich* by Napoleon Hill, I understood that my thinking could make a difference. Until that time, primarily because of the Law of Grace that my parents instilled within me, I thought I just had to accept what happened and react as best I could.

Around 2005, I heard someone say, "You can be, do, or have anything that you desire." I sort of glossed that over, thinking, "Yeah. Yeah. I know all that stuff." Well, that statement turned out to be so true and so powerful that it is hard to believe. And I really did not fully understand it at all, at that time.

So let's take a minute to examine this.

We *have* things and possessions that cost money. We also *have* relationships that do not cost money, yet they are very valuable. And we *have* family; these are people we don't own, but they are our family whether we like them or not. Hopefully, you like your relatives; however, if you do not, I will show you later in this book how to change your feelings toward them so that your relationship with your family no longer has a detrimental effect on you.

How do we acquire any of these things and people in our lives? By *doing* something. Nothing happens until we do something, until we put forth action of some sort: working, talking, selling, driving, studying, reading, listening to speakers, going to college, taking training courses, cooking, cleaning, building, courting, waiting, serving others, writing, loving, and so on.

When we *do* something, the results are that we *have* something: possessions, relationships, cars, homes, toys, friends, family, bigger bank accounts, and so forth.

And we define success by our successful actions that result in us having those things we desire.

How do we know what successful action to do in order to acquire the things that we desire? Somehow, we have to learn that.

In *Put Your Health in Your Own Hands,* I wrote two sections titled, "You are what you eat" and "You eat what you are." The concept is that we act based on "who we are." For example, let's say two people witness someone stumble over a curb and fall on the sidewalk. One of the witnesses is an emergency medical technician (EMT) and the other is an attorney. The EMT knows exactly how to help medically. The lawyer probably does not know what to do medically, yet knows how to help legally. The first and automatic action of each is based on who they are.

Who we are is based on our thinking and the memories of all of our past experiences— good or bad. We are a cumulative composite of everything we have ever experienced. It is important to understand that we can change who we are.

We can eliminate the effects of traumatic events from our past. We can enhance the things that have been good. We can begin to listen to people who are doing the things we desire, and we can model our behaviors after those people who have the things we desire. We can learn from the experiences of those who have been where we are now and have grown beyond that point.

And we can educate ourselves through the help of a mentor or life coach who can teach us to *be* and *do* so that we can *have* the things and types of relationships we desire.

This process of "be, do, have" is very simple and sequential. And it is the reverse of the once-popular paradigm of "have, do, be" that many of us learned.

That old, inaccurate belief says, for example, a person must *have* an education and *do* a good job in order to *be* successful. But, as we will see, this thought pattern is backward to the Law of Co-creation.

First, we must become the person we desire to *be*. The traits of that desired person within us will cause us to *do* the actions that will attract things into our life that we desire to *have*.

If we try to force the actions before we become that person, we will fail because our thoughts and actions will be incongruent and will not have any attractive power.

If we possess things without becoming that person or doing correct actions, we will be very unhappy, living outside of our comfort zone, and we will sabotage our actions or the actions of others around us until we lose our possessions or shatter our relationships, thus forcing ourselves to "go back" to who we "know" we are.

This process of "be, do, have" is so vital to creating your amazing life that I recommend you read this section over and over until you grasp how important it is: You must BECOME the person you desire to be, BEFORE you can take the correct actions to gain what you desire.

One of my mentors often said, "This concept takes five minutes to learn and a lifetime to master."

So, regardless of where you are now in this learning/mastering process, remember that you can be, do, or have anything you desire. It is up to *YOU* to learn how to create your life.

To do that, we must first understand how the mind works, which is the subject of the next chapter.

Worrying does not take away tomorrow's troubles, but
it does take away today's peace. — Marcel Proust

3

The Mind—
Conscious and Subconscious

We live in two worlds: the physical world of the body and spiritual world of the mind. And we have two minds: the conscious mind that rules our physical world and the subconscious mind that is in charge of our spiritual world.

The conscious mind can handle only a limited amount of information, only what is coming through our five physical senses at that moment. Therefore, it is very much the *now* of what is happening at this instant. This means that, like the small end of a funnel, only a small, fixed amount of information can go through it at one time.

Think of the conscious mind like Doppler radar. It might show your local weather; however, there is much more weather—perhaps, something very dramatic—out there beyond what is visible on the screen. People who are not aware of anything other than what is going on in their conscious, visible, objective, concrete worlds don't have "the whole picture." It is as if they are "asleep" to the world beyond what they can see.

The subconscious mind pertains to the invisible world beyond the immediate view on the radar screen. It is a storage mechanism for everything we have ever seen, heard, tasted, touched, smelled, or imagined. Everything that all our ancestors have experienced is stored there as our genetic memory.

The subconscious mind is like the large end of the funnel. It can handle millions of functions at one time. It is the part of the mind that controls all of our "automatic" physical body functions, and it manages all of the cellular and chemical functions within our bodies.

Because the subconscious part of our minds operates within the invisible spiritual dimension, we understand that in that world there is no time. We can think forward into the future and backward into the past. There is also no space. We can imagine something very large or very small in an instant. This part of our mind is not limited by the three dimensions of space: height, width, and depth or the fourth dimension: time.

Our link that connects the physical world of the body and the spiritual world of the mind is our awareness of being. This awareness of being exists in the invisible world of spirit where God exists. When we increase our conscious awareness, then that unlimited part of the mind is no longer subconscious, but rather it becomes inner conscious. We can begin to use this infinite store house of information to intentionally create an amazing life.

Sleep is the natural state of the subconscious mind. When we physically go to sleep, the subconscious part of us awakens and continues to function even though we are not aware of it. The subconscious mind is responsible for our dreams.

Similarly, intuition and "psychic" information comes into our conscious mind from the subconscious when our conscious mind is turned off—when we are sleeping, meditating, or performing those monotonous, automatic tasks that do not require focus, such as showering, driving, running, cycling, or daydreaming.

The word "psychic" bothers some people. Let me assure you that, in my experience with many, many patients, precognitive experiences are a normal phenomenon for the great majority. A great number of people have had the experience of knowing who is calling on the phone before answering it, thinking about someone who calls a few minutes later, or knowing or dreaming something will happen before it happens.

In fact, this mental/emotional activity is our nature, part of our survival system. But most of us have underdeveloped this trait or not developed it all, probably because we have been taught that either this trait is evil or not scientific. It is as though we have the ability to read but either do not have books or are afraid to open the books we do have.

Let me give you an example of a precognitive dream. Six times during my life, I have dreamt about someone driving a hearse. Each time, except once, within two weeks, the person in my dream who was driving the hearse died. When I dreamt about my father driving a hearse, I was able to get him into a doctor who discovered a brain tumor, which was treated, and my dad lived for eight more years.

If the conscious mind is limited and the subconscious mind is so infinite, it makes sense to me that we need to learn as much as possible about how to make the subconscious mind work for us.

Because there is so much evidence that these subconscious phenomena do occur often, should we not ask: "If we can use our mind to create an amazing life, why do most of us not have everything that we desire?"

The reality is that we do. Everything we currently have in our lives, we have created in some way, consciously or subconsciously.

We might not want to believe this, especially if our lives are a little messy, but the truth is that what we are experiencing now is what we have been thinking about or feeling in the past. Or to say it another way, "If you want to know what you've been thinking about, look at what you are experiencing right now."

4

There is a formula for getting ahead and creating an amazing life

The first step to the formula is to change how we remember the past. Let me tell you what that means.

We have created everything we are now experiencing. Remember that we function in one of those three paradigms: Law of Karma, Law of Grace (Let go and let God), and Law of Co-creation.

If there are things in our lives we do not like, it is not because we are here to learn karmic lessons or settle the score with other souls. It is not because we are being punished for past sins or are bad or not in a state of grace.

Most of us have created our lives in innocent ignorance. We do not know what we do not know. We do not know that we can create an amazing life. We do not know how to create an amazing life. We do not know the formula. Some of us do not even know there is a formula. The formula has been discovered and written about many times for thousands of years; however, the majority of people still do not know, understand, or use this formula.

After 35 years of study, trial and error, starting and stopping, pain and joy, I have found a formula that works for me. Will this work for everyone? Yes, I believe it will. It is so simple that I believe it can work for everyone who applies it in the prescribed manner. This formula has three parts and all of them are "secrets" that have been known and used by successful people for a long time.

Until now, they have not been taught in this manner, so now you will learn the shortcut to get ahead more quickly and easily.

A few years ago, I attended a medical conference. One of the topics was compliance with the frequency with which prescription medicine is actually taken. The presenter used some simple research. Medicine was dispensed in a bottle with a computer chip in the cap. This chip recorded every date and time when the bottle was opened. The results showed that medicine prescribed once per day had a fairly good chance of being followed; medicines prescribed twice per day were less likely to be taken accurately; and medicines prescribed to be taken three and four times per day were never taken as directed. The presenter also claimed that 40 percent of prescription medicines that were called into a pharmacy were never picked up. I think that percentage is a little high, but I see this situation all the time. People seek and pay for advice every day, but often do not follow it. When one offers advice to someone who does not seek it, that advice is almost never followed.

Why is this? We are humans. All of us operate on a set of mental programs that have brought us to this point in our lives. We have established a comfort zone on which we can rely. And we are often reluctant to try something new, because every time we do, we generate anxiety with a subconscious desire to return to our comfort zone. Becoming aware of this concept will help us move past the anxiety we associate with change.

I once worked with a young woman whose husband physically abused her and their children. Frequently, she would call me after he had beaten her. Once I asked her, "Why don't you just leave him?" She replied, "I don't know where to go and, at least, here I know what to expect."

I was astounded! However, this appears to be the plight of many people who simply do not know that this type of hopeless, fearful thinking promotes and prolongs the situation. Most of the time, they just do not know how to think hopefully, positively, or correctly enough to get themselves out of a bad situation.

Actually, before we can use this formula for creating an amazing life, we must awaken to the fact that *change is possible*—and that *we are responsible* for those changes. If we desire change in our lives, we are going to have to make some changes. Nobody is going to do it for us. There is no white knight coming to our rescue. There is no superhero to save the day. We must do it ourselves.

The key point of what we must learn is simply this: Change begins in our *conscious* mind, which must take control of those old thoughts and change those imprisoning memories that are programmed and stored in our *subconscious* mind.

This is a simple formula. It is a recipe that is less complicated than taking medicine once a day. Most people can follow this formula, but many will not. Those who will do it, will accept and own these ideas and make them believable. My job in the next few pages is to show you how doable this formula is.

5

Is there something about the past that YOU can change?

If our present lives are not exactly what we desire, there are only two reasons:

1. We are allowing thoughts from the past to hold us back. More accurately, **memories** from our past are holding us back.

2. We are not thinking correctly about the future.

Remember, it is not the actual past event that holds us back; rather, it is the memory of the event that affects us. To be successful, to get ahead in any area, and to create an amazing life, we must change how we remember those past traumatic events. This might not be easy, but you can do it, especially when you have the correct tools.

"I am more and more convinced that our happiness or unhappiness depends more on the way we view the events of life than on the nature of those events themselves."   — Alexander von Humboldt

---

Most of us are full of "mind viruses," a term borrowed from Richard Brodie's book, *Mind Viruses*. It means that we carry thoughts and old mental programs that are no longer useful or have been innocently or purposefully implanted into our minds. These mental malfunctions come from those past physical and emotional events that create outdated programs that no longer serve us.

Where do these mind viruses come from? They are programmed into our memories from our past experiences. My friend Lee Carroll calls them filters. These filters are like putting on a pair of glasses that modifies what we see. One set of glasses may change the color of what we see. Another could make everything wavy. As we go through life, we have put on many pairs of glasses that alter our vision. The pure thinking of our innocent minds at conception is now altered by the presence of thousands of these filters. They cloud our ability to think clearly.

Mr. Carroll explains that they come from five sources: Growing up, spiritual concepts, gender, logic, and professional. These filters create *images* in our minds, *words* in our heads, and *feelings* in our hearts and "guts." They permanently alter our thoughts unless we change them. It is important to understand that these memories by themselves are not really good or bad. They are just things that have happened to us. How we interpret these memories is what can have a detrimental or beneficial influence on our present thinking and, therefore, limit or enhance our ability to get ahead and have an amazing life.

Here is a simple explanation of these five filters.

First, Growing Up filters. This group of filters will vary widely depending on where you were born, the personality of your parents, the beliefs of your parents, their hobbies, their income, and social status. These filters are also formed by the political climate of our growing up years, our parents' political views, and where we went to school.

Let me give you a subtle example of how small past events from our growing up years can have a major harmful impact on our lives today.

> Someone I know, who I will call Lawrence, has a life that I do not consider to be very successful. He currently lives by picking trash and reselling "good stuff" and metal that others throw away. When Lawrence was about 10 years old, he was helping his father with a building project. They were putting wood siding on a shed that the father had built. The father really did not expect too much of the 10-year-old boy, but he was trying to teach his son some things about building and carpentry. Lawrence was left-handed, not really very coordinated or mechanically inclined, and things were not going well. Around every nail that Lawrence pounded into the siding was a rosette of hammerhead marks. The dad, in frustration, said, "We are done here. Why don't you just go fishing?"

Fishing was something Lawrence loved and was very good at. Off he went to a small trout stream. An hour or so later, he came back with a gigantic rainbow trout, over 40 inches long. It was so big that he could hardly carry it. The father was ecstatic and very proud of his son's trophy fish and bragged to everyone who would listen. The family was poor and they could not afford to have it mounted, so they did the next best thing; they stored it in the freezer to be able to show it off.

The unfortunate result of this experience was that Lawrence received so much praise over this event that he adopted this as a lifelong coping strategy. Every time there was stress, he would go fishing, hoping for the big one. Countless jobs ended like this. If there was too much pressure on a job, he would "just go fishing" and never go back to work.

Lawrence's unsuccessful strategy for life began innocently with some very simple activities and circumstances over which the boy had no control.

Here's another seemingly insignificant event that created long-lasting effects.

My patient, "Alton," with a lifetime of weight issues, attended Overeaters Anonymous for a while. During one session, he became aware of a memory of an event from his past that contributed to his obesity now. At age four or five, he was visiting his cousin whose family was in the business of potato farming. On this visit, Alton's aunt baked a three-pound potato, and he ate the whole thing. The aunt, grandmother, and mother all praised him lavishly for several days. Comments like: "Good boy," "You are such a big boy," "That is amazing to be able to eat like that," and "You will grow up to be a strong man if you eat like that," created a filter that caused Alton to love potatoes in every form and crave starchy food during times of stress and need for approval.

Anyone who has been molested, raped, humiliated, beaten, or physically and mentally harmed as a child will carry filters that modify their current thoughts with fear, caution, mistrust, and so on.

Many times, these filters are produced by experiences with those we love and who are supposed to care for us. So now we are stuck with a very negative experience connected with someone we trusted, such as a parent, teacher, minister, doctor, sibling, friend, and so forth.

Fortunately, most of us have dealt with most of these memories, filters, and programs and can function fairly well in our families and in society. But some of us are limited by these memories so that we are stuck and cannot reach our full potential. Many times when we try to change, it feels threatening because the filter was created by some powerful person from our past and we may have been very small and powerless when it was created.

The second filter is Spiritual. This group of filters comes from our past spiritual experience and teachings. Some people have no experience with any form of spiritual teaching. Most of us who have some spiritual teaching may have learned that God is a large supernatural entity outside of ourselves who controls all aspects of our lives and is a judgmental parent who will punish us if we do not follow all the rules.

Depending on your spiritual influences, you may or may not have been taught to ask questions such as: "Is there a God? Is there a God who has created the Universe and predetermines all of our life experiences? Is this creator of the Universe benevolent or judgmental and ready to condemn us to eternal hell?

We generally accept our parental teaching until we come to some age of discernment, then we either accept their beliefs for life or modify them in some way. If you grew up with a belief in a judgmental, vindictive God of the universe, it can make change very difficult if that belief is not congruent with the life you desire to create. It is difficult, not impossible.

The third filter is Gender. What did your parents teach you about men and women? Are you lady-like or a tom boy? A macho man or a femme fatale? A hunter or shopper? Who are your role models for men and women? What are your gender roles for professions and household jobs? Do real men wear pink? This filter may be clouded by unpleasant past experiences with a "bad" husband or wife. Hormones play a definite role in our gender feelings. Most of us have been conditioned that God is male. Most religions are patriarchal. Why are "nature," the "Earth," and man's "hot car" referred to as "she"? All of these filters have been put in place by someone. At some point, we have to deal with the validity of these concepts.

The fourth is the Logic filter. Our beliefs and thoughts must make sense. Our "logic" is often not really logic but beliefs and opinions based on our other filters. Is something real or not real? Most of our logic comes from what we have seen or read. Sometimes it comes from what we have seen on television or on the internet. These things may or may not be real. This question must be answered about everything in our lives before we can move into a paradigm of co-creation. Sometimes we simply have to agree to disagree.

The fifth is called the Professional filter. What we have learned in school and professional training is a filter. The professional filter works well with the growing up filter. We all want to be accepted and follow the rules. We often worry about what people will think of us if some new concept does not fit with our professional training.

Every filter that we currently accept has been brought to us by someone we trusted, respected, and loved. A parent, a sibling, a teacher, a clergyman. If someone tells us something different or wants us to modify our beliefs, change can become very difficult because the filters are put in place by someone we loved, someone who was doing the best they could at the time. Even if the filter is outdated, its source makes change difficult. Even so, change is possible and usually desirable.

These five sets of filters and many more create our personality. We do not want to change them all. We generally have no need to change most of them. But some of these concepts and things that we believe are not accurate, and in order for us to move forward and get ahead and create an amazing life, they must be changed.

Some events in our past affect all of our filters. An experience of childhood molestation will affect everything: Social, Spiritual, Gender, Logic, and Professional. Clearing the memories of those events with some of the techniques you will soon learn can have a dramatic effect on your whole life. Think of the five filters as wearing five pairs of glasses at the same time. When you take off some of the old pairs of glasses, you get a new vision of what your life could become. It now becomes clear why it is often difficult to get a distinct picture of what you desire your future to look like. To really create an amazing life, we need to modify some of the filters and remove some, if not all, of the outdated glasses.

"If you are distressed by anything external, the pain is not due to the thing itself, but to your estimate of it; and this you have the power to change at any moment."
— Marcus Aurelius Antonius

These detrimental filters are viruses in our minds, infecting everything we do. Dr. Wayne Dyer tells in his book *Excuses Begone* how he sent an email requesting people to submit mind viruses they had or were experiencing. Of over 5,000 responses, these were the most common:

1. It will be too difficult.
2. It is going to be risky.
3. It will take a long time.
4. There will be family drama.
5. I do not deserve it.
6. It is not my nature.
7. I cannot afford it.
8. No one will help me.
9. It has never been done before.
10. I am not strong enough.
11. I am not smart enough.
12. I am too old (or not old enough).
13. The rules or the government will not let me.
14. It is too big. I am too fat. I am too small.
15. I do not have the energy.
16. I have a family history of …
17. I am too busy.
18. I am too afraid.

Please understand why what I am saying here is so important. When we think, we generate a vibration within the DNA in every cell in our body. This vibration is transmitted out, much like the signal from a radio transmitter. Scientists used to think this transmission came only from the brain and that others received it as "thought waves." Quantum physicists have since discovered that the vibrational frequency is transmitted from every cell in the body and this vibrational frequency changes in accordance with the thoughts in our mind. The mind virus contaminates our thinking and changes our vibrational frequencies, which affects others as a negative non-verbal message.

We are transmitters and receivers of vibrational energy.

I am sure you can recall times when you met someone new and either you wanted to hug that person or you wanted to run and hide. This feeling of attraction or fear was created within you by the vibrational frequency transmitted from the other person. The effect you felt within your body was based on your memories of similar vibrational frequencies that came from the memory of old events (good or bad) and old "mind virus" programs.

Let me give you some examples:

- If you are going for a job interview, you will not get the job if your body is vibrating mind virus frequencies such as: "I am not smart enough." "I am too old for this job." "I am not worth the money they are offering."

- It will be very hard to build a long-lasting, trusting, faithful relationship with someone if your DNA is vibrating mind viruses like: "I am an alcoholic." "I don't trust women." "Men always leave me. "I am too fat to be loved." "My relationships never work out."

- And it is very hard to be healthy or manifest perfect health, if your mind is thinking: "I am too old." "I have a family history of heart disease." "I am a diabetic." "I have cancer." "I get the winter flu every year." "I get sick every time I go on vacation." "I catch every virus from my children." "The doctor told me I have one year to live."

- Similarly, it will take a long time to sell a house if you are vibrating incongruent frequencies. Some people claim they buried a small statue of Saint Joseph upside down in the front yard and sold their house the next day; they say that is a miracle and divine intervention. I believe the scientific explanation is this: The sellers changed their thoughts from worry and doubt to hope and certainty. That change created a new vibrational frequency that, like a magnet, attracted the correct buyer who was also resonating with that same frequency.

When we "own" mind virus beliefs, they, in turn, own us and are expressed in our bodies. We might genetically inherit tendencies or predispositions toward one disease or another, but it is our beliefs that, in part, cause us to have a certain vibrational frequency that allows and enables these genetic tendencies to be expressed in our bodies. Bruce Lipton in *The Biology of Belief* introduces the new science of Epigenetic. He clearly shows that our thoughts can modify our physical health by turning genes on and off. The foods we eat and toxins we ingest are other factors, all of which I discuss in detail in my book *Put Your Health in Your Own Hands*.

When I was a boy, a child in our neighborhood was kidnapped. My parent's words were, "Aren't we lucky we are poor. We will never have to worry about you kids getting kidnapped." This mind virus instills a belief that poverty is good and safe. This obviously was not accurate, but the fearful child may accept it as true and, often, never updates the program.

When we encounter such negative, inaccurate mind viruses, we must treat ourselves with mental surgery or with mental medication to remove those viruses, filters, and all beliefs about ourselves that are not accurate.

"Your task is not to seek for love, but merely to seek and find all the barriers within yourself that you have built against it." — Rumi

---

6

The first step in the formula—change the memories of your past

We are now at a point where we get the idea that we can change our lives, that we can get ahead, that we may be stuck here and now but not forever. We also begin to understand that we will need to change the detrimental memories of the past.

The first step in the formula for creating an amazing life involves becoming aware of:

- our current mental and emotional state,

- the words we use to describe our life situation, and

- memories of past events that are still negatively affecting our life today.

The process to implement the first step in the formula includes:

- tools to release past emotions,

- various methods to revise the memory of negative past events,

- ways to perform mental surgery to remove the mind viruses, and

- the use of natural remedies to assist change.

"There are only two mistakes one can make along the road to truth; not starting and not going all the way."
— Buddha

Awareness – the steps of change

Once you begin this process of making your life better, be sure to continue it. Any attempt to change is usually accompanied by anxiety or even fear. Therefore, the formula requires that we begin by simply acknowledging that there might be—and probably are—thoughts and memories that are causing us to be stuck in the past.

Prior to even wanting to change, we were in a state of *unconscious incompetence*. In this state, we do not know, and we do not know that we do not know.

When we become aware of our desire to change, we enter the stage called *conscious incompetence*. This occurs when we know that we do not know and feel a desire to know.

With persistence and practice, we move into the state of *conscious competence*. Here, we know what to think and what to do, but we have to constantly generate conscious thoughts that will keep us moving in the correct, desired direction.

Ultimately, we reach the state of *unconscious competence*. This occurs when we have eliminated the mind virus and reprogrammed our thought process so that positive thinking is firmly implanted and automatic. After that, the old mind viruses fade from our awareness, and we no longer use them as a strategy for living.

Timeline of Traumatic Past Events

As you become aware and decide to change the memories of past traumatic events, you will need to create a timeline of your past. This is a list of memories of events and people associated with those events that are holding you back and keeping you from creating the life you desire.

But, before I relate more about this timeline of past traumatic events, please be aware that good things from the past also affect our lives.

> When I was in the sixth grade, my teacher caught me flying paper airplanes in class. She dragged me by the ear into the hall and said some very important life-changing things to me. She said, "You are a leader and people will follow you. No matter what you do, good or bad, people will follow. So you must think very hard now about what you are going to

do. Do you want good things to come to you or bad things? Those are your choices." This was a positive experience that still resonates with me today. I do not know what she saw in me, but I am grateful for how she handled that situation.

Likewise, as you create your timeline of traumatic past events, you might also make notes about positive events that happened in your past. That positive list isn't the focus of this exercise now because we are, instead, emphasizing how to rid ourselves of the memories of past traumatic events. But later, as you move into the state of conscious competence, you might look at that list of good things that happened to you to build competence and confidence.

Now think about your past. List the memories, without reliving the trauma, of as many past unpleasant events as you can. The timeline might include:

1. **Grief, Loss, Broken Attachment of Any Kind**. This can be the death of a family member or a favorite pet. It could be the loss of a job or missed opportunity. I know a couple who built their own log home. They cut and peeled and cured and notched all the logs by hand themselves. It took over three years to build that house. A few months after completion, a faulty appliance started a fire and burned the home to the ground. Neither have been well since.

2. **Lost Love, Real or Imagined, Loss of Romantic Relationship.** This is somewhat like grief; however, subtly different. It has to do with loss of a romantic, sexual relationship. This can be real, actually being dumped by a soul mate, or it can be imagined. "Brandi," a teenage patient, was in love with a rock star in a band that she had never seen live. She had all his music and paraphernalia. She had never met the man in person. Yet, when he married someone, she was crushed for months. She needed some counseling and homeopathic remedies to help her return to a normal life.

3. **Abandonment, Forsaken Feelings, Helplessness.** These feelings arise from real or perceived abandonment. This can be related to a recent situation, or it can be related to an abandonment event from childhood. A child might be contaminated with abandonment issues because his or her parents were separated during the pregnancy. This also applies to people who might be homeless or have no resources. This definitely is a factor in the emotions of children of divorce with an absent parent. Some people were abandoned by parents who were alcoholics, ill, or worked all the time. Adopted people frequently suffer from this issue.

4. **Mortification, Humiliation, Embarrassment, Guilt; Being Teased, Bul-**

lied, or Raped. The emotional events that cause health problems in this category have to do with events in which people were very embarrassed or humiliated. Rape can fit into this category. Someone with a birth defect who was teased relentlessly might be affected throughout life by these kinds of events. I care for a man in his forties who wet his pants while giving a little speech when he was in the fourth grade. He had magnified that event into something bigger, instead of minimizing it, and it has affected him his whole life.

5. **Fright.** People of any age can have frights. The effects of these usually subside gradually; however, sometimes they can continue to cause problems. I once saw a little boy with stuttering problems. After taking a careful history, the story unfolded that the boy also had fear of bright lights and preferred to sleep in total darkness. The cause of this was related to a visit to a hospital emergency room after a fever seizure when he was two years old. When he regained consciousness after the seizure, extremely bright lights shining in his eyes in the ER left him with a general anxiety and phobic reaction to bright lights. Homeopathic remedies resolved both the stuttering and the fear of the bright lights.

6. The Shock of **Bad News.** What is the worst bad news you can think of? For some, it is the death of a family member. For others, it is the diagnosis of cancer or some other serious health problem. The shock of bad news can have dramatic effects, but this can be removed with homeopathy and with the simple techniques I will share later in this book.

7. **Worry, Anticipation of Bad Things Happening, Performance Anxiety.** Some people have a mental habit of finding the worst in a situation. Some always look for the worst case scenario. A minister at one of the churches I attended a few years back gave this good advice: "Pray the solution, not the problem." People who can consciously take their mind off the bad and mentally play simulations of what they would rather have instead will soon create a new habit of looking for the best outcome.

8. **Disappointment.** This can be a subtle emotion and is often cumulative from years of disappointment, usually from childhood. The child who is promised a trip to the ballpark, the dance, or the zoo but cannot go due to the parents' other obligations will often lose trust in the parents as well as other authority figures and spouses. Other disappointments such as not winning a contest, not being given a role in a play, not being accepted into medical school, going through bankruptcy, or missing an opportunity are often devastating.

9. **Overexertion of the Mind, Emotional Excitement, Burnout.** Many children and adults suffer from this emotional situation. Often these people are diagnosed with ADHD or anxiety disorders. I once had a six-year-old patient with severe anxiety. The history revealed that his mother nearly died from a reaction to a medication during the child's birth, and he nearly died as well. This separation from his life source instilled severe chronic anxiety, which was successfully treated with a homeopathic remedy.

10. **Anger, Real or Suppressed.** It is important to understand that the emotion of anger is normal and actually a good venting tool. The trouble comes when the anger stays for a long time or when it leads to violent actions. Some families use the Five-Minute Rule. This is very simple. It is okay to be angry; however, it can only last for five minutes. After that, it is time to forgive and forget. Holding anger releases some chemicals into the blood that are very damaging to tissues and greatly accelerates aging.

11. **Homesickness, Empty-Nest Syndrome.** Many people do not realize the devastating effect this can have. Sometimes, there is a period of homesickness when children leave home. Usually they get over it within a few weeks or months; however, some suffer for years. Often a child experiences homesickness when uprooted if the parents move to a different town for their work or military reassignment. Parents also experience similar emotions with empty nest syndrome.

12. **Jealousy.** This is a huge emotional block that some people carry their whole lives. The negative impact it has on the body chemistry is subtle yet very powerful. Often, over time, this emotion becomes chronic. It will eventually attack a person's genetically weak system, leading to the production of illness, not to mention the years of unhappiness that are associated with retained jealous feelings.

13. **Dishonesty, Theft, Loss of Integrity.** Most people have some event from the past that involves taking something that they did not own. This can lead to feelings of guilt, shame, and embarrassment. We need to make restitution, if possible. This can be done anonymously or just done mentally if physical repayment is not possible. Then we must forgive ourselves and move on. Later, I will present a formula to release these negative feelings forever.

Write Your Timeline

Now that you've read through this list of traumatic memories, stop reading and write your timeline if you have not already done so.

Go back to the preceding list as often as necessary. Use it to jog your memory, looking for emotional and physical events that might be stopping you from moving forward in your life.

This exercise is necessary. If you do not do this part of the formula now, you are not ready to read and receive the rest of the information in this book. I understand and have been in your shoes. Sometimes, we just do not want to face that dragon again. So, be aware that is not necessary to relive that past event, just name it. Often we think we have successfully buried the past, but it is still an anchor attached to our ankle, keeping us emotionally stuck at the age at which the event occurred. This is why some adults act like three-year-olds.

So, please, put the book down and write your timeline **NOW**. Just do it. You do not have to think about them; just list some memories of the events of your past. If the big events are too painful, list some "smaller" ones and release those first.

Below is an unedited letter from a patient who used this technique. This story might help you overcome your hesitation to write a timeline.

> After dealing with chronic hives for over 18 months and some great advice from a friend, I made an appointment to see Bob Huttinga.
>
> I have learned that my body does not react well to any synthetic medicines so when I had heard Mr. Huttinga PA used homeopathic treatments, I was very excited. A while into my appointment I could tell right away that the Lord had sent me to where I needed to be, to finally get the help that I needed. The hives were discussed and a treatment plan was established. Which I must say after three weeks it is working great.
>
> Also in my appointment Mr. Huttinga could tell there was more going on with me than I even was aware of. He asked if I was dealing with any grief and I had to admit that my dog had recently passed away unexpectedly and that I was still grieving over the loss of my Dad, gone 27 years and my Mom, gone 12 years. He suggested that I write them a letter. What? I thought. He explained the benefits of putting your thoughts down on paper and then after reading it aloud and then burning the letter, this will help me to allow myself to let go of the grief and start moving on. That these emotions may be adding to the chronic hives. So I thought what the heck I would try it.

You see I needed to make some medical decisions for my mother near her end and to this day I always questioned if I had done the right thing by her. I would remember that scene in the hospital every day. So I wrote my parents a letter and told them I was sorry if I had caused my Mom any undo suffering and that the decisions that I made I felt were right at the time. Then with time you question that. I also told them that I needed to forgive myself and start living life the way they taught me to....with no regrets. I told them that I loved them and to please watch out for my dog that had come to them recently. That I was really going to try to let go of the bad memories and fill that space with good ones instead.

To my amazement two days later as I finished my prayers and was climbing into bed I realized that today I did not relive that horrible day. That I didn't even think of it once. I was amazed! The letter worked for me and my grief. I know now that I may have thought it was a bit strange to do this but I have written more letters since. To my husband, friends and even my dog. The load feels lighter, the shoulders more relaxed and even a lot more days of "hives free." Who would have thought that writing letters to those that we love, we miss, even to those that are still here and have unresolved issues, would do so much good for the heart, the body, the mind, and the soul.

Thank you, Mr. Huttinga, for everything you have done for me. I thank God every day for healers like you.

PR 6-1-15

Use Your Timeline

Once you have written the timeline of traumatic emotional events in your life, you can begin to reprogram those events and change how they affect you from this point forward.

Remember that you cannot change your past. However, you can change how memories of your past affect you today and in your future.

There are a number of good methods for reprogramming memories of old events to make these changes. Here are some releasing, healing exercises that have helped me and that I recommend for you.

Write Emotional Release Letters

Write letters to anyone with whom you might have had any conflicts. This usually includes parents, bosses, spouses, ex-spouses, children, someone who abused you, or someone you might have hurt. It can also include old friends or anything or anyone who has bothered you in any way. Very likely, you will write some letters to yourself. You may also write to a diseased part of yourself, a body part that you do not admire, a house that will not sell, or a car that keeps breaking down. I know, this sounds weird, but read on. You will understand soon.

Write your letter with a pencil on paper. Tapping your fingers on metal typewriter keys or a plastic computer keyboard does not imprint the information in your brain in the same way that writing it longhand does. So, handwrite it, please. The letter can be 10 pages or two paragraphs, and anything in between is acceptable.

At the end of the letter, add the following statement: "I will no longer carry this debt for you physically, mentally, emotionally, or spiritually."

Then add: "I love you. I bless you. I release you. I forgive you for everything I think you have done to me."

It is important to write these endings exactly as they appear here.

Read this letter, with the endings, aloud three times, and then burn it. Make a release ceremony around burning the letter. Release the smoke to God or the Universe and the ashes to the Earth. Sometimes immediately, but usually within a few days, you will feel internal emotional shifts, either subtly or dramatically. Often the people around you will seem to change.

Write as many letters as you wish until you feel you have released all the old baggage you have been carrying around from the past.

In a week or so, to see if you are still holding onto unfinished emotional attachments, simply think about the person or part of your body to whom you wrote your letter. If you experience any unpleasant emotions, you must write another letter. I once had to write six letters to an individual to remove the emotional effects of a very traumatic event. Had I not removed it, I would have acted unconsciously on those deeply imprinted negative memories the rest of my life.

You might find it difficult to write "I love you" to someone who really hurt you, so think of this as if you are loving all of humanity or all of creation. If at first you cannot write "I love you," skip that phrase and add it back in when you write this person again as you continue to release their memory.

You may write a letter to yourself to release something that you think you did wrong or were embarrassed about or because of a health issue. Write the letter in the same manner and just imagine the letter is to your younger self at the age you were when the event occurred. Remember, you did the best you could at the time with the tools that you had. Then add the ending: "I will no longer carry this debt physically, mentally, emotionally, or spiritually."

Then add: "I love you. I bless you. I release you. Thank you for carrying the guilt and shame for all these years. Now, it is time to let go. I forgive you for everything I think you have done to me."

Read it all aloud three times and burn it, giving the smoke to God and the ashes to the Earth.

When we store impressions of emotional events in our mind, the brain is supposed to minimize them until we eventually forget. And while our conscious mind forgets, the subconscious never forgets and continues to act on that information. In some cases, the subconscious mind will even magnify memories to create an impression of the event that is worse or more traumatic than it was originally.

This is what happens with post-traumatic stress disorder (PTSD). A memory of a traumatic event is stored in our DNA as a vibrational frequency and in the brain as a neurochemical pathway. When a trigger incident occurs, the memory of the original event automatically triggers a stressful fight or flight reaction.

The same situation happens with phobias. If someone has a fear of heights from nearly falling off a water tower, even seeing someone else standing on the edge of a tall structure will trigger a phobic fight or flight, adrenaline reaction in the observer's body.

The letter writing and other techniques I will share will change that reaction so the trigger no longer reacts automatically with "fight or flight" body chemistry.

I have heard hundreds of stories of how releasing these old memories has changed lives, but here are a few.

Three days after writing a forgiveness letter to his mother, CJ found his biological father who had also been searching for him.

Less than one week after writing a letter to her house that had been for sale for two years, GL had an offer and earnest money in her hand.

The next day, after PM wrote and burned a letter to a problem employee, a shift occurred and now this problem employee is the most productive agent in the company.

Within a few days of writing a letter to his wife about her habit of leaving the cap off the toothpaste, HN found that it no longer bothered him.

LD was having uncontrollable grief six months after losing two pets to an infectious illness. Within days of writing letters to the dogs and the veterinarian, she felt the shift as the mourning eased and anger subsided.

Less than a week after writing an emotional release letter to her alcoholic husband, EJ said that he told her he was getting tired of drinking every night until he passed out. She wrote two more letters. She said she felt like she did not care anymore if he drank or not. In less than a month, he stopped using any alcohol.

We know from quantum physics, through a process called entanglement, we are at some level connected to every other soul on the Earth. Some of these attachments are unhealthy because of the memory of the past emotional or physical trauma, but unless we purposefully release that person, we will stay connected in that unhealthy way. These are techniques that actually help us to "Let go and let God."

Here is an unedited letter from someone who has read an advanced copy of this book. Please follow her advice. Do this first step now. I know there is resistance here. Change creates anxiety, and we want to procrastinate or think we are fine the way we are. But you will achieve great peace of mind when you clear some of the old memories by writing, reading, releasing and forgiving the memories of the past.

"As a Happiness Life Coach, I always leave my clients with homework steps in order to help them achieve the results that they wish to enjoy! As I read Bob Huttinga's wonderful book, A *Shortcut to Success*, I followed his three homework steps in the exact order he laid out. I can tell you now that, without a doubt, Step 1 (clearing out the memories of the past by writing release/forgiveness letters) is by far the most important step of the three steps. If one does not complete this first step, one will surely re-create the past over and over again. I learned this the hard way. Now I know better.

Writing letters of forgiveness and release has altered my present experience completely. My mind is mostly healed and I am free to create differently now! I'm happy and excited about today and about my future! Thank you, Bob!" GK 8-15

If writing these letters seems to make no change in your feelings and emotions, re-evaluate to make sure you are doing all the steps: Writing the letter, adding the endings, reading it aloud, and burning it with a little releasing ceremony.

If still no change occurs, use one of the other techniques listed below.

"In forgiving ourselves, we make the journey from guilt for what we have done (or not done) to celebration of what we have become." — Joan Borysenko

---

Re-Vision (Revise the memory of past events)

Another technique is one that I learned from Neuro Linguistic Programming (NLP). This is a tool that takes into account how the body communicates with itself. I call this technique *re-vision*. Vision means to see something. Re-vision or to revise means to visualize something again, however, this time imagine it in a different way than the original event and the mental movie that is stored in the subconscious mind.

Once you have brought the memory or the event to your awareness, replay the memory of that event in your mind several times as if it had happened in a different way. This creates a new optional vibrational frequency in your DNA and a new neurochemical pathway in your brain. Each time you create a revision, you also create another option. This gives your body a chance to change how it reacts. Without these options, the body, which is controlled by the subconscious filters, must continue to react in accordance with the original event. Your body has no choice unless you intentionally give it new options.

It is best to re-vise your memories in a relaxed state, during a meditation, or just before going to sleep. Here is the process I use, personally, to clear past events that continue to affect me in the present.

Get into a relaxed state or a meditation with the intention of changing "the event" in your mind. This is one of those events from the timeline of your life that you feel is still influencing your present in a way that is not beneficial to you. Make sure you will not be interrupted for at least 15 to 20 minutes.

With eyes closed, imagine you are in a small airplane on a runway. This runway represents the time line of your current life. The future is in front of you and the past is behind you. Imagine taking off in your airplane, rising above the timeline. From that vantage point, you can see where you are now as well as the past behind and the future ahead, all at the same time.

Now turn the plane around and go back down the timeline into your past until you are at a time before "the event" that you have decided to re-program. Then turn the plane around again, flying above and along the timeline, going toward the future. As you approach "the event," consciously decide to go around it, passing it to the right. As you do, mentally imagine looking down on a totally different scene from the original. When you have flown past it on the right for a while, rejoin the timeline flying in the direction of your future.

Turn your plane again and go back to before "the event." As before, turn the plane, and once more mentally see the event in your future. But this time, as you approach "the event," fly to the left of it, looking down, imagining it happening again, however, in a brand new way that is beneficial to you. When you have flown past the event, rejoin the timeline.

Turn around again and repeat this process at least two more times, each time imagine that event happening in a completely new way, perhaps with a different color of light or at a different speed.

With four passes, you have four optional pathways that your timeline can take instead of the way you "remembered it." This gives your brain four new neurochemical pathways and your DNA four new vibrational frequencies from which to choose whenever the old emotional trigger is tripped. Because you are genetically programmed to avoid pain and to seek pleasure, you will automatically select one of the "new" memories that you have installed, and the old memory will fade with lack of use.

Scientists have taken some microscopic videos of one neuron disconnecting from one nerve cell and hooking to another. This is called neuroplasticity, a biological phenomenon that proves that how we think, can actually change our anatomy and physiology. This physical change in the neuron pathway changes how we recall information and, therefore, how we react or respond to the trigger from the past event.

Here is an example.

> Years ago, I worked with "Ralph," a man with PTSD from the war in Vietnam. He had frequent flashbacks of events from the fighting there. His life was a mess, having lost his wife to divorce, lost his job due to absenteeism, turned to alcohol to medicate himself at night so he could sleep, and having become very depressed to the point of contemplating suicide. Prescription medications had actually made him worse. The main "event" was walking into a North Vietnamese village with a group of soldiers. An old woman came out of a hut with a large basket of fruit. One of the other soldiers yelled that there were grenades in the basket with the fruit. He immediately hit the dirt and shot the woman with a burst from his M-16. Then, he went into a type of shock when it was determined that there were no grenades. He never received any psychiatric or therapeutic debriefing in regard to this event and was discharged with several medals for bravery less than a month later. However, he felt ashamed and believed he could never forgive himself. He played "the event" over and over in his mind and slowly magnified his memories of the original experience into something greater than it really was. These magnifications became his predominant thoughts every day.

I had him do four revisions in the manner that I described earlier, each time creating a new scene. One time, the old woman came out with a bunch of flowers all in plain sight, without the basket. Another time, she came out holding up a bunch of grapes. Another time, she had a stick with which she attempted to strike at Ralph, but he took the stick and broke it over his knee. In the final scene, he imagined that she had come out of the hut with arms open and gave him a hug.

One month later, he could barely recall the original event. His anxiety slowly decreased. He got his job back and his wife eventually remarried him. This simple revision, done just one time, gave his mind and body options, new neuro-chemical pathways, and new DNA vibrations. He now had choices, no longer limited to one point of reference.

Revision is a very powerful tool. Use it on any memories that you feel are detrimental to your mental and physical health. You can use it on current physical and emotional traumas that occur in the present. We call this, "Re-create your day." At the end of each day, replay any event that did not go the way you would have preferred. Imagine that event happening the way you desired. Doing this simple procedure will prevent the negative events from becoming memories that might have detrimental effects in the future.

"Let no sleep fall upon thy eyes till thou hast thrice reviewed the transactions of the past day. Where have I turned aside from rectitude [integrity]? What have I been doing? What have I left undone, which I ought to have done? Begin thus from the first act and proceed; and, in conclusion, at the ill which thou hast done, be troubled, and rejoice for the good." — Buddha

---

2500 years ago, Buddha taught the same concept of reviewing your day. I would go a step further and, instead of being troubled by the things that did not go right, revise them mentally. Re-create your day.

Below is a very short book by Portia Nelson, *There's a Hole in My Sidewalk.* It gives an example of how we can revise our thinking and avoid the same old pitfalls over which we have stumbled in the past.

"I walk down the street.
There is a deep hole in the sidewalk.
I fall in.
I am lost... I am helpless.
It isn't my fault.
It takes forever to find a way out.

I walk down the same street.
There is a deep hole in the sidewalk.
I pretend I don't see it.
I fall in again.
I can't believe I am in the same place.
But, it isn't my fault.
It still takes me a long time to get out.

I walk down the same street.
There is a deep hole in the sidewalk.
I see it is there.
I still fall in. It's a habit.
My eyes are open.
I know where I am.
It is my fault. I get out immediately.

I walk down the same street.
There is a deep hole in the sidewalk.
I walk around it.

I walk down another street."

— Portia Nelson

Using the steps in the formula in this book will shorten that learning process considerably. You will not have to fall in the hole so many times before you learn the lesson, and you will be able to get ahead sooner and live an amazing life longer.

The Mental Enema

Sometimes we are unable to find what may be holding us back and keeping us from getting ahead. I have used the following exercise, which I call the mental enema.

Get very relaxed in a quiet place where you will not be disturbed for a few minutes. Close your eyes and imagine you are standing in a shower stall. Now imagine plugging a large hose into your ear and feeling it flushing all the bad memories and limiting thoughts out of your body through the bottoms of your feet and down the drain of the shower. You can make any version of this that you like. This is a great general cleansing tool for hidden mental and emotional memories that are out of your awareness.

Clean up your language

As you move through the process of conscious incompetence and conscious competence, you will begin to listen to your language. You will hear yourself use words that, in the past, unconsciously fueled those mind viruses.

It is time to do mental surgery to remove those mind viruses.

You will begin to limit your use of those words, phrases, and figures of speech. And, eventually, you will remove them permanently from your daily language.

You will find yourself using positive language to express your condition or situation. Many cancer survivors, for example, claim that their illness was a "blessing in disguise" that brought about a "positive change" in their lives or in their relationships with others.

With this in mind, become aware of the words and figures of speech that people commonly use. Do you see yourself in these?

Statements that can impact your health: He/she is a pain in the neck/butt. I would give my left arm for ______. I am sick and tired of ______. That galls me. That fries my ass. I can't stand ______. That situation gives me such a headache. The traffic is so aggravating it gives me a gut ache. That really pisses me off. All I have to do is look at food and I gain 10 pounds. I would give anything to ______. That is going to be the death of me. That kills me. That is so irritating. That knocks me out.

Statements that can impact your self-esteem: I hate ______. I feel so stupid/ dumb. I am a loser. You idiot. You fool. Who do you think you are? You Dummy. Silly me, I _____. I am just a _____. You know me, I screwed up again. Any phrase in which you put yourself down.

Statements that can hinder your success: I will try. I can't. I have no idea. I never _____. I always _____. I can't believe that. Good things come to those who wait. The only luck I have is bad luck. Everything I touch turns to crap. I can't afford _____. Money doesn't grow on trees. Like usual, I _____. I just can never get ahead. I am waiting for my ship to come in. Someday I will _____. I know I could never do it, but I wish _____. Pride goes before a fall.

Most of these words and phrases are things we heard our parents or close relatives say, usually with innocent intentions. But they have literal and figurative meanings, and our body cannot tell the difference between a seemingly innocent observation and a request for results. "All of these statement are limiting in some way because they tell your body and subconscious mind something that is not true. You must do mental surgery to remove all of these sayings from your language. These negative affirmations are contaminating your life. Instead, make a statement like this, "Everything I touch turns to gold."

Remember also to keep weak words out of your daily language; these words indicate activity but do not lead to accomplishment, and activity without accomplishment is futile. "Try," for example, implies an attempt but suggests failure. "Want" literally means lack because, when you want something, you are in a perpetual state of achieving but never receiving; saying "I desire" is much more effective. "Healing" is a weak word because it implies movement but not attainment. Rather than praying for "healing," pray for perfect health because asking for healing never really demonstrates to the invisible world of the inner conscious mind how perfect health looks, sounds and feels.

Stop telling your sad story. If something bad happens, like getting a flat tire, missing a flight, having a car accident, or the like, do not tell anyone. Every telling of the story magnifies the negative emotions attached to that event. The more you tell your story, the more your DNA vibrates that information, more people also vibrate that information, and you are more likely to attract more events that cause those same unpleasant emotions.

Beware of the statement, "Everything happens in threes." Believe it or not, that is a creative statement through which we unconsciously create three negative events in quick succession. This saying should definitely be removed from our memory, and we should cancel it every time we say it or hear someone else say it. Alternatively, we might use a similar—but significantly different—

statement to create more good things in our lives: "*Good* things always come in threes."

My old mentor, Dr. Bruce Bennett, used the term "Litany of Laments" or an "Organ Recital" when patients came to the office with many complaints or when he heard them reciting their history to someone in the cafeteria. Stop telling those stories and do not refer to any illness as "*my* headache" or "*my* ______." When you profess to own that condition, it is more difficult for your body to remove it and return your health to normal.

Again, I offer this advice from my own experience. I recall telling my tales of woe to anyone who would listen until someone kindly pointed out that this only kept me stuck in the negative past. Do as I do when an unfortunate event occurs: Do a quick revision of the event in your mind, see a positive side of the situation, and let the negativity go as soon as you can. A good friend of mine says, "Life is like a book, just turn the page and read on."

Here is one final item on this topic. Please, stop watching the news and reading every sad story in the newspaper. Some of those stories are toxic and are contaminating your memory. Most of the news is not something you can fix. It is not your business, so turn the news off, selectively read the newspaper, and maybe use Google News to scan headlines so you have limited exposure to material that detract from your amazing life.

"Life is overflowing with the new. But it is necessary to empty out the old to make room for the new to enter."
— Eileen Caddy

Affirmations for Health

Affirmations are words that we hear repeatedly that get imprinted into our memory and operating systems. Positive affirmations can be used to reprogram the mind viruses. The following statements correspond to the mind viruses that Wayne Dyer talked about in his book *Excuses Be Gone*. He created some of these, and I added to some of them.

I recommend that you read these into your smart phone or a recording device. Listen to them and read them aloud several times each week. As they become part of your normal thought process, you will only need to reinforce them occasionally.

1. I can do anything I choose to do. I choose to do it now. I eat anything I choose and remain slim, trim, and toned.

2. I enjoy being my true self. For as long as I can remember, I have always had plenty. My life is filled with abundance, and I am filled with gratitude.

3. I will do whatever it takes for as long as it takes.

4. I have loving support from those who care.

5. I am okay. I deserve a wonderful life. Joy and happiness are my birthright.

6. I am learning to overcome any genetic and old, learned programming. My thoughts are healing my body quickly and easily.

7. I am connected to unlimited sources of abundance. I have always had and now have and always will have plenty. In my life, there is abundance for all.

8. The right people are already here to help me with my quest. There are always great people looking for the opportunity that I have.

9. I guide myself at all times to do the things and say the things that lead most to my success and my perfect health. I am creating a new healthy body and everyone loves it. More importantly, I love it.

10. I have access to unlimited assistance. I am not my body. I have physical, mental, emotional, and spiritual strength to accomplish any task I desire.

11. I am a co-creation of myself and the Divine. All is perfect and I am a genius in my own right. I am wise and exercise perfect timing. Everything I touch has a beneficial outcome.

12. My experience and enthusiasm guide me and I learn easily to create my new future quickly.

13. I function well within the rules of society, making adjustments for my circumstances. I am connected to everyone and everything.

14. I think only about what I can do now. I think in small, manageable pieces to accomplish great things.

15. I am filled with passion and excitement for my new life. I am filled with vital energy every day. My mind is sharp. My thoughts are precise and clear. My body is slim, trim, toned, and healthy.

16. I release all events of the past and live fully in this present time with joy and love. I am creating a new past in which I have a perfectly healthy body, brain, and mind.

17. I easily find the time for the beneficial things in my life. I accomplish tasks quickly, easily, accurately, and efficiently. I easily find the correct path and purpose for my life.

18. I accomplish anything I put my mind to. I release unhealthy memories of past experiences with gratitude and move forward with joy and enthusiasm. For as long as I can remember, I am in control of my body and my life. My future is bright and filled with promise and purpose.

Use Natural Remedies

There are some great natural remedies to help release events from the past: Homeopathy, Bach Flower remedies, and Essential Oils.

Homeopathic Remedies to Remove the Effects of Emotional Shocks

Homeopathy is a complete therapeutic system of specially prepared medications that are dissolved in the mouth. It is based on the use of natural remedies that for 200 years—long before prescription medications—people have effectively used to maintain optimal health.

While the entire system is somewhat complicated, I've written a brief description and recommendations in my book *Put Your Health in Your Own Hands*. Another book, *Homeopathy for Professionals and Laypeople* by Blair Lewis PA-

C, is a good starter for those interested in basic homeopathy.

In the list below, I've included some of the homeopathic remedies that can be of great benefit for people with memories of past events that are affecting them and blocking their progress now. These are the same events that I listed earlier in this book in regard to creating your timeline of memories of past events.

- **Grief, loss, broken attachment of any kind:**
  Ignatia, Natrum Muraticum, Aurum Metalicum

- **Lost love, real or imagined, loss of romantic relationship:**
  Ignatia, Natrum Muraticum, Staphysagria

- **Abandonment, forsakenness, helplessness:**
  Aurum Metalicum, Natrum Muraticum, Pulsatilla, Aurum Muraticum Natrum, Bach Flower Gorse, Agrimony

- **Mortification, humiliation, embarrassment, guilt, being teased, bullied, or raped:**
  Colocynthis, Staphysagria

- **Fright:**
  Aconite, Gelsemium, Ignatia, Staphysagria, Lycopodium

- **The shock of bad news:**
  Gelsemium, Ignatia, Natrum Muraticum

- **Worry, anticipation of bad things happening, performance anxiety:**
  Argentum Nitricum, Gelsemium

- **Disappointment:**
  Aurum Metalicum, Ignatia, Staphysagria, Lycopodium

- **Overexertion of the mind, emotional excitement, burnout:**
  Aconite, Pulsatilla, Chamomilia, Coffea, Lachesis, Bach Flower Elm

- **Anger: real or suppressed:**
  Bryonia, Nux Vomica, Lachesis, Chamomilia

- **Homesickness, empty-nest syndrome:**
  Aurum Metalicum, Ignatia, Bryonia, Staphysagria

- **Jealousy:**
  Lachesis, Apis Mellifica, Nux Vomica

- **Dishonesty, theft, loss of integrity:**
  Natrum Muraticum, Staphysagria

For our purposes here in this book, use these remedies in the following way. Select the remedy for the condition you desire to change. At the health food store, purchase the remedy in a potency between 9C and 30C depending on what they sell. Any potency in that range will work. Place one pellet under your tongue once or twice a day until you feel the changes in your emotions. Sometimes it takes a few days and sometimes a month. The labels on the containers usually say to use 3-5 pellets per dose, but one pellet works just as well as five and costs less.

Because of how they are made, it is not possible to have side effects from homeopathic remedies. However, you can experience an aggravation. This is a temporary worsening of your symptoms. If this happens, it simply means that you have the correct remedy, but it is too strong. Just reduce the frequency or the potency of the remedy and continue to use it.

Some people feel the need for some professional help with using homeopathy. Ask at your local health food store. They usually know the area practitioners.

Bach Flower Remedies

Dr. Edward Bach, a physician in England, has developed a series of 38 homeopathic remedies made from flowers. These have many uses and are very effective natural treatments. More details about each remedy can be found on The Healing Center website: www.thehealingcenteroflakeview.com/bach_flower_remedies.html.

For our purposes today, the best remedy for those who are stuck living in the past is Honeysuckle. Here is Dr. Bach's description of this remedy: "For those who live much in the past, perhaps a time of great happiness or memories of a lost friend or ambitions which have not come true. They do not expect further happiness such as they have had."

For most effective use, place five or six drops in a 32-ounce water bottle and sip on that throughout the day. Do this for two to three weeks until you forget to take it or until you feel like the memory of the past event is no longer influencing you.

Essential Oils

There are many essential oil blends that help with emotional healing. The one we find to be most effective among people with stuck memories of past events is "Forgiveness," made by Young Living Essential Oils.

Before going to bed at night, place one drop of Forgiveness oil on the skin around your navel and gently massage it in, using clockwise motions. Again, do this daily for two to three weeks, until you forget to do it, or until you feel the event diminishing from your memory.

While massaging the oil into your skin, think about a situation in which forgiveness is needed: to forgive another or to forgive yourself for past choices. Do not force yourself to forgive the person or yourself at the beginning, just use the oils daily until you are ready to release that anger and resentment. When done in this way, your actual act of forgiveness will be easy and permanent.

Summary

Regardless of what method or technique we use, when it comes to removing old emotional obstacles from our past: We must learn to clean up our past. We must learn to take out the trash. We must clean the garage. We must reorganize the basement of our minds. We must turn our fear into faith. We must change doubt into certainty.

"If the only tool you have is a hammer, you tend to see every problem as a nail." — Abraham Maslow

---

You now have many new tools. You can use any or all of the suggestions. You can use the mental/emotional techniques while using the natural remedies. Remember this is a process and continue to affirm to yourself, "Every day, in every way I am getting better, better, and better."

7

The second step in the formula — clarify your goals and desires

---

The second step in the formula is to clarify your goals and desires.

In this step, we must think about the content of our goals. We are not yet going to focus on the process of how we will arrive at the goal, but I am going to teach you how to fine tune this process of imagining and visualizing your desires. To clarify, imagination is the creation of a mental image of something new that you have never seen or imagined before, whereas visualization is the replay of a mental image of something you have previously seen or imagined.

Clarifying your goals is the second step in the formula to getting ahead and creating an amazing life. It would be started only after you have cleaned up some of your past limiting memories.

Please understand that clarifying your desires and learning to think correctly from the future before fixing the past will do you no good. That would be as ineffective as stepping on the gas pedal of your car before starting the engine.

Failure to complete step one before doing the second step is one of the reasons that many people found that the concepts presented in *Think and Grow Rich* and *The Secret* were not completely effective. They tried to place the cart before the horse, and that simply does not work. Drying your hair before taking a shower is an incorrect and ineffective sequence.

In this step, we will learn how to think about our desires and clarify them.

Remember what Earl Nightingale said, "We become what we think about most of the time."

Our minds are creative. This does not mean that we are creative only in the areas of music, art, writing, poetry, and so on; it means that our minds literally have the ability to create our experience.

The word "create" means to bring something into existence. Richard Bach, author of *Hypnotizing Maria*, describes it like this, using some made-up words:

> Thought creates Imajons. These come together to form Conceptons. There are Positive Conceptons, which are Exhilarons, Excytons, Rhapsodons, Jovions, and Negative Conceptons, which are Gloomons, Tormentons, Tribulons, Miserons. These Conceptons form clouds which become probability waves which vibrate at tachyon speeds which become the holograms of our lives.

You might need to read this paragraph a few times to understand the concept. Go back now and read that again. Thoughts create imaginings that become concepts, positive or negative, which become clouds that become waves that vibrate at speeds greater than light, which manifest into who we are, what we do, and what we have.

An outcome always begins with an idea, a simple thought. Put this into a more practical scene. Most of you have, at one time or another, purchased a car. Let's examine that process. First, there is an idea. For some reason, you decide that you need or desire a car. Your desire may be of three different types:

1. Your desire might be vague or general, like you need reliable transportation—any car will do.

2. Your desire might be very specific with exact details of color, make, model, engine size, and so on.

3. Your desire might be just a feeling associated with buying a car—feeling great, sitting behind the wheel, checking out your reflection in the store windows as you drive down the street.

The idea must gather momentum. In order for enough momentum to grow to critical mass, you must have a really good feeling about this vehicle. If there is not a good feeling, if there is any fear or doubt, you can never get enough momentum to create the car. It will always remain an idea, just a thought. If, however, the thought grows large enough over time to reach critical mass, you begin to attract, like a magnet, the people and situations that will bring the car to you. When the critical mass is enough, the right car will find you.

> I once saw a Smart Car by Mercedes Benz in a movie and said, "I like that. Someday, I am going to own one of those little cars." Occasionally, after seeing one on the street or in a movie, I would re-affirm my desire. I attached no specifics to it. Although, because I'm tall, I did stop at a dealership in Denver to look the car over and sit in it to make sure that I could get in and out of it comfortably.
>
> One day, probably two years later, while driving to work, I saw one parked on the roadside with a "For Sale" sign on it. Excited, I called the number only to be told that a few minutes before the car had been sold to someone who had looked at it the day before. I was disappointed, but again reaffirmed my desire, "Someday I will own and drive one of those little cars." The next day, we left for a two-week vacation. The day we got back, I saw that the car was back on the side of the road again. This time, I stopped at the owner's house and spoke with him. It seems the man who had bought this little car had bought it for his wife for a birthday surprise only to find that she did not like the car. He had brought the car back, and "magically" it again appeared in front of me. I immediately bought the car, this time for $500 less than the original price.

I became the owner of a really nice Smart Car just by thinking about owning it. Of course, some action and money were required. But please understand that the action and the money are the least important part of the creative process. When done correctly, after the critical mass of thought is compiled, you will be guided to have effective action and do whatever it takes until your goal is present in your physical reality.

> On the first day of 2015, Barb and I were writing goals for the year. She wrote, "I desire to have a different car this year." She never buys new cars. We always find great deals on slightly used ones. Three days later, Barb had an accident with her car. Neither she nor her passenger were injured, but the car

was totaled by the insurance company, and she is now driving a newer, better car. This law of co-creation works. We do not have to know how, just that it will work and does work all the time.

This is the process by which we create every part of our lives. Most people have never thought about this in this way. And even if you have heard of the concept of the Law of Attraction from books like *The Secret* and *Think and Grow Rich*, you might still not know how to make it work. How many times have you wanted something and not received it? How many times have you felt disappointed and given up?

In this book, I will show you how to change that. Read on, and you will learn how you can be, do, or have anything you desire.

Some time ago, Barb and I taught a workshop called 21 Ways to Find Peace. This was based on the material produced by author Byron Katie. One of the things she teaches is that we need to mind our own business. Ms. Katie says that there are three kinds of business: Your Business, My Business, and God's Business.

God's Business has to do with the big things that we really cannot control or change. Things like the weather, earthquakes, hurricanes, and so on. If we worry about them, we create acidity and inflammation in our own bodies. We can take some action and pray for the people involved, we can donate money, and we can even volunteer our time to relief efforts. But when we catch ourselves thinking and worrying about these big things, we need to stop for a minute and say to ourselves, "This is God's business and He will take care of it." Then just relax and let it go.

My Business is anything that directly affects me. I must pay attention to and take care of those things. They are my responsibility. Only I can fix them. For example, if I smoke and it is causing health issues, I am the only one who can correct that situation. No nagging from friends and family will make that change. And God does not care. He will help if we ask correctly, but He will not interfere if we insist on continuing with detrimental behaviors. If I am behind in my property taxes, only I can fix that. If I do not, someone else—the government—will step in and take care of it for me. I must take care of my own business.

Your Business is the stuff that only you are responsible for. If you don't take care of your yard, it is your business. If I am upset about that, that is my business. It is not my business to fix your lawn or try to make you fix it, but it is my business to look at myself and how I react. My anger can make me ill, but it does nothing to you or to your lawn. I should only give advice or express my opinion on your business if you ask. Otherwise, it is best if I stay out of your business.

Many of us have grown children and we still think it is our business to run their lives. Let up. After your children reach the age of 16 or so, your responsibility is done. If they make what you perceive as "mistakes," they have to be responsible for them. Let them be. Do not meddle. Love them, pray that they will find their path, and let them go on their merry—or not so merry—way. It is not right if we take away their lessons and their chances to learn from what they do. Remember children learn by what they see, not from what they hear.

We all have lessons to learn. Most of us have to learn to "live and let live." We must take care of our own business and let everyone else take care of theirs. If we spend our time taking care of our own business, we will be healthier and more at peace. Try it. Practice. Every time you find your mind in God's business or someone else's business, step back and let it go. You will begin to feel less anxiety and more peace in your mind and body. You will be healthier and happier.

Your goals and desires for the future should be your business. You have to set a goal in order to achieve any outcome. Most people never begin this process. A few years ago, as Barb and I were getting ready to leave on a vacation to Hawaii, several people said to me, "You are so lucky. We can't afford to do that." The truth is, I am lucky, but not in the sense that most people mean. My definition of luck is: "Priorities and Planning Meet Preparedness." Barb and I decided about two years earlier that we wanted to take a trip to Hawaii because neither of us had been there before. We set that as our priority. And we began to plan! We saved money. We watched for special deals on airfare and accommodations.

So think about this process. You make a decision to do something. In your mind, you see yourself there, and you automatically begin the creative process. If you never decide to go, nothing will ever happen. So, the first step is the choice to do it. Set the goal.

The next step is to ask: how much *moolah* are you going to need to make this happen. This is preparedness.

Money is also called *currency*. Like a current in a stream, it implies flow and movement. Money is a renewable resource. In order for money to do something for you, it must move and go somewhere or to someone in exchange for what you desire. Currency does neither you nor anyone else any good in your pocket. But to take a trip, you need to accumulate some *deniro* to exchange for that trip. You do not want to pay for this trip on a credit card. Save upfront so the entire trip is all paid for when you go. Then the memories of the trip are not ruined by the stress and regret of having to pay the credit card bill.

Let's say you need $5,000. For most of us, we look at that and feel overwhelmed. We often think, "I just do not have that kind of money. You are lucky to be able to afford that, but I cannot afford it." So look at your budget. Ask yourself, "How can I afford this?" Where could you squeeze out a few bucks each month to begin accumulating some *jing* for that trip?

Here are a few places in our daily lives where we could make some changes. Some people smoke at, let's say, $5.00 per pack, which is $150 per month or $1,800 per year. If you go out for dinner to even a modest restaurant or to the movies once a week for $30, you are paying out $1,500 per year.

I used to party once a month or more and easily spend $50 each time so that is $600. Most people spend $50 to $150 per month on cable television. If you cancel that service and turn off the tube, at the average rate you have another $1,200 per year. How many of us buy doodads all the time, junk that we do not need? Many of us spend $2 to $5 per day for coffee and snacks. That's another $1,000 per year you can save by packing a lunch instead of eating out. *Ka-ching*. Once you look, there are lots of possibilities.

So, you have the three Ps: Priority, Planning, and Preparedness.

Once you decide to go on your trip to recharge your solar batteries and see the world, you must make some priority decisions to budget the flow of your currency into the trip fund—or whatever special fund you choose. It might take two or three years to build up your "fun" fund, but it will be well worth it.

When you begin thinking like this, things happen. Barb and I found a great deal on a cruise that was half the usual price. That happened because we were prepared, not because we were lucky. You can experience something like that too—if you're "lucky" in the "priority, planning, preparedness" sense of the word.

Changing your thinking like this is also great for your health. You eliminate a bunch of really bad, unhealthy habits and convert them into life-changing, mind-expanding experiences. Enjoy the ride.

So begin to think about your desires. Sometimes they just seem like dreams that could never come true. But to clarify them, you must write them down. At first, this might seem too big. If you have cleaned out some of the past limiting memories and mind viruses, it will be easier to think that your dreams can come true.

Write a bucket list or a set of long-term goals. These will be things you desire to do and places you desire to see and people you desire to meet before you die. It is good to have 50 or 100 items on that list. When you do this, your inner conscious mind works in the background to bring those adventures into reality. I recall saying as a small farm boy in Montana that I would like to climb the pyramids in Egypt someday. I did not think of it often, but every once in a while, the thought would float through my mind. Some 50 years later, that dream became a reality. If I had never stated this as a dream or desire, it would never have happened.

Write down with pen on paper, not with a computer, short-term goals in the following areas: family and relationships; occupation, job and career; recreation and fun; money, income, savings and retirement; and health and fitness.

These must be written in positive terms. Our subconscious mind cannot focus on the reverse of an idea. If I say, "Do not think of a purple bear," you instantly construct a mental image of a purple bear. This also happens with the negative version of goals. We cannot help but focus on what we are lacking and what we do not want to experience. And you guessed it, that negative version is the exact thing we will create in our lives. As you write these goals, use a little trick called "begin with the end in mind." Write them as if you have a magic genie who will grant you unlimited wishes. As you write, do not judge the goal whether you think you can or cannot have it or do it. Just write it. You can edit these goals later.

- **Family and relationships**
  Write goals for all relationships, not just romantic relationships. Think of children, parents, employers, customers, friends, the clerk in the store, and everyone who you deal with.

- **Occupation, job and career**
  Write goals for your career, doing something that you love to do. Describe the characteristic of the job or business. Inside or outside work? How many hours per day? Per week? With

people or alone? Easy or challenging? Creative or routine? Different each day or the same each day? Regular or flexible schedule? Working days or nights?

- **Recreation and fun**
  Write goals for your recreation and fun. Travel or stay at home? Outdoors or inside? Alone or with others? Adrenaline or relaxed? What things and toys are important to you?

- **Money, income, savings and retirement**
  Write goals for your income, savings, and retirement. How much money would you like to make per year? How much are you going to save per paycheck? What are you going to do when you retire? How much money are you going to give away? When? To whom? What will be your monthly income when you are retired?

- **Health and fitness**
  Write goals for your perfect health. What is your ideal body shape and size? What age are you going to be when you pass away? What year will it be when you pass away? How much exercise are you going to do? What kind of exercise are you going to do? What is your nutrition going to be like? What kind of natural medicines and supplements can you take to achieve perfect health?

Take some time to answer these questions as well as ask questions of your own. Clearly write some goals that may be long-term and short-term. Make no judgment and do not try to figure out how these things could happen. Remember, you're creating that amazing life. Write these goals as if you have a magical genie who will grant your every wish. Write as if you are already there, experiencing that desire. When you attempt to determine how these things will happen, doubt and fear begin to creep in. This pours water on the fires of creation. Do not tell anyone else about your goals. That will definitely pour water on your sparks of creation.

Your goals are the prophecies of what someday you will become. — David Camron Gikandi

---

8

The third step in the formula— think correctly from the future

The third step is to think correctly from the future.

We have been told by the ancient masters how to think. But this technology of thinking correctly has not been taught in our schools and churches. So, most of us do not know the details of this final step.

Here is the third step to the formula: Each night, just before going to sleep, get comfortable, lie flat on your back, inhale and exhale three deep breaths, relax your body completely, and create a movie in your mind. In this mental movie, imagine whatever it is that you desire. And do this as if it were already completed. Insert a feeling of gratitude. Imagine shaking hands with someone. Imagine that you are being congratulated for what you have accomplished or that you are thanking someone for helping you achieve your desire.

After you go to sleep, your subconscious mind awakens and leaves your body. It goes out into the spiritual world of the subconscious mind to find ways to accomplish your desire. It locates the people, negotiates the deals, and creates the timing that will bring into existence your desire. After you do this, you might become aware of new ideas. You might receive intuitions and guidance. You might meet someone who can help you. All these things nudge you in the direction of your desire until it becomes an accomplished fact. There is a time delay on this guidance as well as the manifestation of the desired outcome. How soon it happens is determined by how well you have cleaned up the limiting memories of those past events that affect that particular goal or desire.

> Barb and I live upstairs above The Healing Center. When guests would come to visit us, we had to run downstairs to open the garage door to let them in. One day I said to her, "We need an extra garage door opener. So when people come to visit, we can just push the button to let them in." The next afternoon, someone gave me a garage door opener as payment for a favor that I did for him.

Is that creation or coincidence? After doing it many times, I believe it is co-creation.

Play this mental movie each night just before going to sleep. Do this regularly until you feel your desire is a certainty. Sometimes when you awaken, you will be surprised that what you desire has not already happened.

Here are some key concepts to understand before you begin:

- We only have now. The past does not exist. Only memories of our past exist. The only reality is now. When creating our desire, we must learn to think from the future as if it exists now or is already a memory in the past.

- Here is the sequence of events of how things happen. Our conscious mind comes up with ideas. Our subconscious mind is unable to judge right or wrong. It has no discernment. Our subconscious mind does exactly what we ask it to do. It is like a loving spouse who will do anything we ask; however, it is not a slave or servant.

- The subconscious mind implements these ideas exactly as we present them. Implementation depends on the strength and clarity of the thought. Remember, every thought is really two thoughts: The first part is our desire, and the second part is our fear that what we desire will not happen.

- Our thoughts need momentum to be implemented into reality. Spaced repetition adds to momentum. Remember when you were in love? How often did you think about your beloved? Recall Earl Nightingale's greatest secret, "We become what we think about most of the time."

- What do we think about most of the time: our desires or our fears that we won't get what we desire?

- Feelings associated with the thoughts are important for the momentum. The feeling "I am" is stronger than "I am going to." And the feeling "I have done something" is stronger than "I am doing something." The feeling of "already done" is much stronger than "doing it now."

- Thinking *from* something is more effective than thinking *about* something. Thinking as if it is already completed is most important.

- A feeling of gratitude **is a must**. Gratitude always means that something is already completed; if it were not completed, we would not feel gratitude. Therefore, holding that feeling of gratitude greatly accelerates the creation process.

- You can measure positive or negative momentum by how you feel. Remember, every thought is really two thoughts: our desire and the fear of not obtaining that desire. What are you feeling: Goodness, happiness, gratitude, abundance or fear, worry, lack? I recall a saying, "God does not hear what you say, but what you feel."

9

Using the formula to get ahead and create an amazing life

"We cannot solve our problems with the same level of thinking that created them" – Albert Einstein

---

This information sounds redundant, and it is repeated on purpose. This information is so important that I will repeat it several times more so it gets programmed into your brain.

This is a formula. It is a recipe that works. Do all the steps in order. Doing them out of order does not work. You cannot drive down the road before you start the engine of your car. You cannot send an email before you turn on your computer.

Do these steps in the following order:

First, do mental surgery on the memories of your past. Remove the mind viruses. Create a timeline of all events that were not what you would have preferred. Begin to write emotional release letters. Forgive everyone you think did something wrong to you. Revise every detrimental event that you can think of. Mentally ask forgiveness of everyone who you think you have wronged. Forgive yourself for things you have done that were not the smartest choices. Do mental surgery in your language and your stories. Stop adding in new negative events like those broadcast on the television news. Remember to re-create your day every night.

Use the following natural remedies: Homeopathic remedies to release old blocked emotions (review the list of remedies that help specific emotional blocks). Take the Bach Flower remedy Honeysuckle to let go of the past. Apply the Essential Oil blend Forgiveness to release, forgive, and forget memories of the outdated past. These remedies will move you into the freedom of a future without carrying any excess baggage.

Remember to forgive is to forget. Not everyone agrees with this. I suggest you pay attention. After you have written and burned a letter, revised an event, and forgiven those involved, go back a month later, and try to remember it. At best, it will be vague.

Second, think about goals and desires for your future. You must know what you desire to experience. You must write that down to clarify it. This is like putting an address in your GPS. If you do not put an address in that search field, you only have a map of where you are at present, but you have no guidance to get where you desire to go. If God cannot see your desire clearly, how can you expect divine help?

We must clarify what we desire to be, do, and have. How many of you know how to clarify butter? Yes, we just have to add some heat and soon the butter melts and separates into clear and cloudy parts. In our life, sometimes a little heat will help us clarify what we really, really desire. If something goes wrong, do not be disappointed, sad or quit. Simply realize that your goal is being clarified so that you can say with conviction, "No! That is not what I desire; but this is what I really, really expect to experience instead." Then, play your mental movie of your desire as if you have already accomplished it.

"In the face of every problem, breathe and say to it,
'Thank you for being in my life. You are a testament to
my creative power ... now watch me transform you into
a blessing" – Dennis Merrit Jones

Then view this new desire as your new goal, a new goal that just got clarified by the heat of that negative event. With this new understanding, that event will not ever become one of those events that negatively impact you. It will just be something that helped you to clarify your desires.

Third, just before going to sleep, create a mental movie. In this movie, imagine what you desire as if it were already completed. Insert a feeling of gratitude. Imagine shaking hands with someone. The handshake might symbolize one of two things: You are being congratulated for accomplishing your goal or you are thanking someone for helping you achieve your desire.

Repeat the mental movie each night just before sleep until you get to a point when you awaken in the morning with surprise that your mental movie is not yet a reality. When you feel a certainty that it is created, you can start on another project.

This thinking process is the actual mechanism for creation of every part of our lives.

We can stop this creation process with a counter intention. For example, when a hen lays a fertilized egg, the laws of nature dictate that it must hatch in 21 days. That incubation process can be stopped by allowing the egg to cool too much, to overheat, or by stepping on it. Be wary of mind virus thinking from the past that can stop the creation process: "I want a car, *but* I cannot afford it," "I want a great marriage, *but* I do not trust men," and so forth.

That is why you must clean up the past. When there are no obstacles (blocking thoughts or memories from the past) that are holding you back and you are thinking correctly from your desire, it is easy to create an amazing seemingly magical life.

> JR is a patient whose husband passed away four years earlier. She had completed her grieving and had already written some emotional release letters and burned them, clearing much of her old baggage. But she was still lonely and wanted to remarry. She had dated a few men, yet she really was not attracted to any of them.
>
> One day when she was in my office, I told her to write a list of ten characteristics that were important to her in a husband and a marital relationship. I told her to take the words on the list and turn them into a mental movie just before going to bed every night until she felt like her creation project was completed.
>
> About two weeks after beginning this process, she got an urge to go to the dating web site Match.com. On that site, she met a man from a nearby city and started a short-distance relationship. A few weeks went by, and they were getting along nicely. Then, he asked her for money. Of course, warning flags went up and she called Match.com, which told her they were aware of reports from other women from whom he had asked for money, and they had already removed his listing. They also told her that he was not using his real name.

This is a very kind lady and she began to worry about the men who had the actual name that this guy had been using. She went online and googled the fictitious name and found two men with that name, both in distant states. She called one of the men. When he answered, she related the whole story. This led to several long phone conversations and many emails back and forth. Eventually the two met and, sure enough, he had all the characteristics she had put on her list two months before.

She did not marry this man because he became ill and died not too long after their initial meeting. These circumstances, however, did lead her to meet someone else nearer to her home. He also had all the characteristics on her list. As of this writing, she is in the process of moving to his city. She is very happy and much healthier than she was before this started.

Was it a coincidence that a fraudulent man came into her life and happened to use the same name as another man who happened to have the traits she desired in a husband? Skeptical people might say yes; however, I know from my own experience with thinking correctly about the future that this was not an accident or blind coincidence. Events of this sort are **created coincidences**. This is what I call co-creation—you and God bringing a plan *together* in an amazing way.

Co-creation is very simple; we often think it is too simple. Sometimes we want to complicate the process. That is why there are just three steps: Clean out detrimental memories of the past, clarify our desires, and imagine and visualize our desire as if we have already done it.

I have had several Christians tell me that my explanation for co-creation is wrong. They tell me that it is God who decides and delivers those experiences in His timing. I agree; however, we must tell God our desires with a very clear statement of those desires and with a true feeling of gratitude. When our desires are not contaminated by our outdated filters, negative memories, and fearful beliefs, they can become physical reality very quickly. Faith, certainty, and gratitude are the emotions required.

The fact is that every prayer is answered. The questions are: How did we pray and for what did we pray? Did we pray from our past with fear and doubt or from the future with faith and certainty, as if it were already done? Did we pray our desire with faith that we already had it or from our fear that we would not receive it?

God wants us to have our desires. So, are we begging, whining children with no clear understanding of what we really desire or do we present our case to God with clarity and definiteness of purpose?

Mishaps are like knives that either serve us or cut us, as we grasp them by the blade or the handle. — Herman Melville

---

10

Can you create an amazing life for someone else?

The answer to that is a resounding NO.

People always ask me this. They want to help their friends and relatives.

The truth is that each and every one of us is on our own path. Some are searchers and some are followers. Some are producers and some are drifters. Some are workers and some are here on vacation. It really does not matter. We are all here on our own path.

Often, people have an awakening experience that shifts them out of being a passive drifter into an active producer, and they begin to create their own lives instead of being a pawn in the lives of others.

After reading this book, you are likely to be more awake than you were before reading it. However, some will read this and say, "That is BS," and move on with their lives as they were before.

No worries. As I said, each and every person is creating his or her own path, either knowingly or in innocent ignorance. I have wasted many hours trying to help people who were neither seeking help nor ready or willing to make any changes.

In my work as a physician assistant, I often see people who are seekers. I will use words and phrases that they recognize because they are searching. Sometimes I will ask them if they are aware of or have read certain books. If they are on a searcher's path, we will develop some special rapport.

Everyone already has a creative process that works for them. Some creative processes work very well, producing their desired outcomes. Some creative processes work very poorly, with undesirable outcomes. It is not my place to attempt to change that, to judge where others are on their path, or to think everyone should be on the same path as mine. I only give advice if I am asked; however, I will sometimes recommend books or CDs that will be awakening for some people. But, ultimately, I believe everyone is responsible for their individual self just as I am only responsible for my own self.

Often, when someone finds a creative process that works well for them, they become a zealous missionary, feeling they have to convert everyone else around them to their way of thinking. This is a good way to lose a lot of friends. Your co-creation process is for your personal use only. If you want to share the formula in this book, do that only with someone who "gets it" and is also working on themselves. My father always said, "Live and let live." Fix yourself first, and then share with those who are also looking for ways to improve their lives.

Fear and doubt can be created in you by those who are not ready to be responsible for their lives. They do not think you should be so bold as to think you can create an amazing life for yourself. Did anyone ever say to you, "Who do you think you are anyway?" If that happens or has happened, write that person a letter; add the endings about loving, blessing, releasing, and forgiving that I wrote about earlier in this book; read it with the endings; and then burn it. Everyone must create their own amazing life for themselves. If we are not actively doing this, we are drifters who are pawns in the lives of producers who are using us to create their amazing lives.

All that being said, there is a chance that you might be able to influence others to help themselves; however, you cannot do that by nagging, pestering, and criticizing them. If you really want to help people who are important to you, use the formula in this book with them. Write an emotional release letter to them. Read it three times and burn it. Clarify in your mind what you think would be in their best interest (it must be in **their** best interest, not yours). Then, just before going to sleep, make a mental movie of them accomplishing that goal. In your mind, congratulate them on their success. If you awaken during the night and think about this person again, briefly replay your mental movie before drifting back to sleep. Do this a few nights and then forget about it. If they are ready for change and just need a little boost, they might accept your vibrational message and the change will proceed naturally.

Yesterday I was clever, so I wanted to change the world.
Today I am wise, so I am changing myself." — Rumi

Remember, you must present your message as if it were in their best interest, not yours. If they are not ready, they will not recognize the vibrational match and nothing will happen. However, a very interesting thing will happen to you. You will find that whatever actions they were doing or statements they were making that bothered you will no longer be an issue for you. You will realize that you have just created a happier and more amazing life for yourself. If they do something with the new vibration, that is up to them.

I Love
you   GAMU
Aab
PoPa

11

Summary—You are creating your life, make it amazing

You are carrying in your own pocket the matches with which the fires of adversity are being touched off and the waters with which those fires can be extinguished is at your own command and in great abundance.
— Napoleon Hill

This, again, is intentional redundance. We learn by spaced repetition. Once more, here is the formula with the correct sequence.

First, clean up the past. Make a timeline of your life. Write, read, and burn emotional release letters. Revise every event from your past that was not the way you wished it to be. Mentally forgive everyone who you think did something wrong to you. Forgive yourself for wronging others or for poor choices that you made when you did not know better. Use natural remedies to help clear your physical chemistry.

Second, clarify what you desire to be, do, and have in the areas of family, occupation, recreation, money, and health.

Third, just before sleep, create a mental movie, imagining your desire as if it were already done, and include a feeling of gratitude. Remember to shake hands with someone in your mental movie; this signifies congratulations on accomplishment or gratitude for their help.

That is all you need to do. That is the formula.

It is so simple.

Now go out and use this shortcut to create your amazing life now.

Thank you for reading *A Shortcut to Success!*

Dear Reader,

I hope you enjoyed reading **A Shortcut to Success**. I sincerely hope you went through the process and have begun to create an amazing life for yourself. I have to tell you, I really loved the process of gathering bits and pieces of my life experience into a working formula to help you succeed in any or all areas of your life.

When I wrote, *Put Your Health in Your Own Hands*, I got so many letters from fans thanking me for the helpful information in that book. As an author, I love feedback. Frankly, that is the reason I write practical self-help books and will continue to share information with you in future titles. I love to see the changes that people make in their lives as a result of using the suggestions in these books. So tell me what you liked, what you loved and even what you found hard to believe. You can write to me at bobhuttinga@healingcenter.biz.

Finally, I would like to ask a favor. If you are so inclined, I would love a review of **A Shortcut to Success**. Loved it. Used it. Hated it. It is all good. As you may know, reviews can be tough to come by these days. You, the reader, have the power to make or break a book. If you have the time, here is a link to my author page on Amazon.com. You can find my books and CDs there: http://www.amazon.com/Bob-Huttinga-PA-C/e/B00XW1AO2S.

Contact information

Bob Huttinga PA-C
The Healing Center
332 S. Lincoln Ave.
Lakeview, Michigan 48850
(989) 352-6500 (office)
(989) 352-6273 (fax)

www.thehealingcenteroflakeview.com
bobhuttinga@healingcenter.biz

Other works by Bob Huttinga PA-C:

Book -- *Put Your Health in Your Own Hands*, 2014
CD -- Coaching for Perfect Health
CD -- Christian Coaching for Perfect Health
CD -- Fit, Clean, and Sober
CD -- Pay Attention
Newspaper Column -- The Lakeview Area News
Blog -- https://putyourhealthinyourownhands.wordpress.com.